Praise for *Horoscopes for the Dead*
and Billy Collins

"In his latest collection, *Horoscopes for the Dead,* Mr. Collins continues his penchant for writing witty, companionable verse that's often rooted in everyday matters."

—*The Wall Street Journal*

"The best introduction to [Collins's] work since 2005's *The Trouble With Poetry* . . . full of stories that anyone can have, but Collins doesn't so much shine the spotlight as making the moments shine from within."

—*Orlando Sentinel*

"Poetry is one way to understand the universe, but it's often seen as obtuse or pretentious. Billy Collins is one modern poet who has managed to appeal to people who claim to dislike poetry."

—*The Washington Post*

"Billy Collins is a rare poet—accessible and gravid, high-minded and delightful. He is also, quite possibly, the funniest man in po-biz. . . . [*Horoscopes for the Dead*] is vintage Billy Collins."

—Louisville *Courier-Journal*

"One of the things readers love about former U.S. poet laureate Billy Collins's poetry is that it often makes them laugh."

—*Los Angeles Times*

BY BILLY COLLINS

Aimless Love

Horoscopes for the Dead

Ballistics

The Trouble with Poetry and Other Poems

Nine Horses

Sailing Alone Around the Room: New and Selected Poems

Picnic, Lightning

The Art of Drowning

Questions About Angels

The Apple That Astonished Paris

EDITED BY BILLY COLLINS

Bright Wings: An Illustrated Anthology of Poems About Birds
(illustrations by David Allen Sibley)

180 More: Extraordinary Poems for Every Day

Poetry 180: A Turning Back to Poetry

Horoscopes for the Dead

Random House Trade Paperbacks   New York

Horoscopes for the Dead

poems

Billy Collins

2012 Random House Trade Paperback Edition

Copyright © 2011 by Billy Collins

Published in the United States by Random House Trade
Paperbacks, an imprint of The Random House Publishing
Group, a division of Random House, Inc., New York.

RANDOM HOUSE TRADE PAPERBACKS and colophon
are trademarks of Random House, Inc.

Originally published in hardcover in the United States
by Random House, an imprint of The Random House
Publishing Group, a division of Random House, Inc., in 2011.

Library of Congress Cataloging-in-Publication Data
Collins, Billy.
Horoscopes for the dead : poems / Billy Collins.
p. cm.
ISBN 978-0-8129-7562-8
eBook ISBN 978-0-679-60450-1
I. Title.
PS3553.O47478H67 2011
811'.54—dc22   2010018621

Printed in the United States of America

www.atrandom.com

4 5 6 7 8 9

Book design by Liz Cosgrove

for Suzannah

It was the kind of library
he had only read about in books.

—Alan Bennett, *The Uncommon Reader*

Contents

ONE

Grave

What do you think of my new glasses
I asked as I stood under a shade tree
before the joined grave of my parents,

and what followed was a long silence
that descended on the rows of the dead
and on the fields and the woods beyond,

one of the one hundred kinds of silence
according to the Chinese belief,
each one distinct from the others,

but the differences being so faint
that only a few special monks
were able to tell them all apart.

They make you look very scholarly,
I heard my mother say
once I lay down on the ground

and pressed an ear into the soft grass.
Then I rolled over and pressed
my other ear to the ground,

the ear my father likes to speak into,
but he would say nothing,
and I could not find a silence

among the 100 Chinese silences
that would fit the one that he created
even though I was the one

who had just made up the business
of the 100 Chinese silences—
the Silence of the Night Boat

and the Silence of the Lotus,
cousin to the Silence of the Temple Bell
only deeper and softer, like petals, at its farthest edges.

The Straightener

Even as a boy I was a straightener.
On a long table near my window
I kept a lantern, a spyglass, and my tomahawk.

Never tomahawk, lantern, and spyglass.
Always lantern, spyglass, tomahawk.

You could never tell when you would need them,
but that was the order you would need them in.

On my desk: pencils at attention in a cup,
foreign coins stacked by size,

a photograph of my parents,
and under the heavy green blotter,
a note from a girl I was fond of.

These days I like to stack in pyramids
the cans of soup in the pantry
and I keep the white candles in rows like logs of wax.

And if I can avoid doing my taxes
or phoning my talkative aunt
on her eighty-something birthday,

I will use a ruler to measure the space
between the comb and brush on the dresser,
the distance between shakers of salt and pepper.

Today, for example, I will devote my time
to lining up my shoes in the closet,
pair by pair in chronological order

and lining up my shirts on the rack by color
to put off having to tell you, dear,
what I really think and what I now am bound to do.

Palermo

It was foolish of us to leave our room.
The empty plaza was shimmering.
The clock looked ready to melt.

The heat was a mallet striking a ball
and sending it bouncing into the nettles of summer.
Even the bees had knocked off for the day.

The only thing moving besides us
(and we had since stopped under an awning)
was a squirrel who was darting this way and that

as if he were having second thoughts
about crossing the street,
his head and tail twitching with indecision.

You were looking in a shop window
but I was watching the squirrel
who now rose up on his hind legs,

and after pausing to look in all directions,
began to sing in a beautiful voice
a melancholy aria about life and death,

his forepaws clutched against his chest,
his face full of longing and hope,
as the sun beat down

on the roofs and awnings of the city,
and the earth continued to turn
and hold in position the moon

which would appear later that night
as we sat in a café
and I stood up on the table

with the encouragement of the owner
and sang for you and the others
the song the squirrel had taught me how to sing.

The Flâneur

He considers the boulevards ideal for thinking,
so he takes the air on a weekday evening
to best appreciate the crisis of modern life.

I thought I would try this for a while,
but instead of being in Paris, I was in Florida,
so the time-honored sights were not available to me
despite my regimen of aimless strolling—

no kiosks or glass-roofed arcades,
no beggar with a kerchief covering her hair,
no woman holding her hat down as she crossed a street,
no Victor Hugo look-alike scowling in a greatcoat,

no girls selling fruit or sweets from a cart,
no prostitutes circled under a streetlamp,
no solitude of the moving crowd
where I could find the dream of refuge.

I did notice a man looking at his watch
and I reflected briefly on the passage of time,

then I saw two ladies dressed in lime-green and pink
and I pondered the fate of the sister arts,
as they stepped into the street arm in arm.

Who needs Europe? I muttered into my scarf
as a boy flew by on a skateboard
and I fell into a reverie on the folly of youth
and the tender, distressing estrangement of my life.

The Snag

The only time I found myself at all interested
in the concept of a time machine
was when I first heard that baldness in a man
was traceable to his maternal grandfather.

I pictured myself stepping into the odd craft
with a vial of poison tucked into a pocket
and, just in case, a newly sharpened kitchen knife.
Of course, I had not thought this through very carefully.

But even after I realized the drawback
of eradicating my own existence
not to mention the possible existence of my mother,
I came up with a better reason to travel back in time.

I pictured myself now setting the coordinates
for late 19th century County Waterford, where,
after I had hidden the machine behind a hedge
and located himself, the man I never knew,

we would enjoy several whiskeys and some talk
about the hard times and my strange-looking clothes,
after which, with his permission of course,
I would climb into his lap

and rest my hand on the slope of his head,
that dome, which covered the troubled church of his mind
and was often covered in turn
by the dusty black hat he had earlier hung from a peg in
    the wall.

Memento Mori

It doesn't take much to remind me
what a mayfly I am,
what a soap bubble floating over the children's party.

Standing under the bones of a dinosaur
in a museum does the trick every time
or confronting in a vitrine a rock from the moon.

Even the Church of St. Anne will do,
a structure I just noticed in a magazine—
built in 1722 of sandstone and limestone in the city of Cork.

And the realization that no one
who ever breasted the waters of time
has figured out a way to avoid dying

always pulls me up by the reins and settles me down
by a roadside, grateful for the sweet weeds
and the mouthfuls of colorful wildflowers.

So many reminders of my mortality
here, there, and elsewhere, visible at every hour,
pretty much everything I can think of except you,

sign over the door of this bar in Cocoa Beach
proclaiming that it was established—
though *established* does not sound right—in 1996.

As Usual

After we have parted, the boats
will continue to leave the harbor at dawn.
The salmon will struggle up to the pools,
one month following the other on the wall.

The magnolia will flower,
and the bee, the noble bee—
I saw one earlier on my walk—
will shoulder his way into the bud.

Thieves

I considered myself lucky to notice
on my walk a mouse ducking like a culprit
into an opening in a stone wall,
a bit of fern draped over his disappearance,

for I was a fellow thief
having stolen for myself this hour,
lifting the wedge of it from my daily clock
so I could walk up a wooded hillside
and sit for a while on a rock the size of a car.

Give us this day our daily clock
I started to chant
as I sat on the hood of this Volkswagen of stone,
and give us our daily blood
and our daily patience and some extra patience
until we cannot stand to live any longer.

And there on that granite automobile,
which once moved along
in the monstrous glacial traffic of the ice age
then came to a halt at last on this very spot,

I felt the motion of thought run out to its edges
then the counter motion of its
tightening on a thing small as a mouse
caught darting into a wall of fieldstones
on what once was a farm north of New York,

my wee, timorous mind darting in after him,
escaping the hawk-prowling sunlight
for a shadowy cave of stone
and the comings and goings of mice—
all that scurrying and the secretive brushing of whiskers.

The Guest

I know the reason you placed nine white tulips
in a glass vase with water
here in this room a few days ago

was not to mark the passage of time
as a fish would have if nailed by the tail
to the wall above the bed of a guest.

But early this morning I did notice
their lowered heads
in the gray light,

two of them even touching the glass
table top near the window,
the blossoms falling open

as they lost their grip on themselves,
and my suitcase only half unpacked by the door.

Gold

I don't want to make too much of this,
but because the bedroom faces east
across a lake here in Florida,

when the sun begins to rise
and reflects off the water,
the whole room is suffused with the kind

of golden light that might travel
at dawn on the summer solstice
the length of a passageway in a megalithic tomb.

Again, I don't want to exaggerate,
but it reminds me of a brand of light
that could illuminate the walls
of a hidden chamber full of treasure,
pearls and gold coins overflowing the silver platters.

I feel like comparing it to the fire
that Aphrodite lit in the human eye
so as to make it possible for us to perceive
the other three elements,

but the last thing I want to do
is risk losing your confidence
by appearing to lay it on too thick.

Let's just say that the morning light here
would bring to any person's mind
the rings of light that Dante

deploys in the final cantos of the *Paradiso*
to convey the presence of God,
while bringing the *Divine Comedy*
to a stunning climax and leave it at that.

Good News

When the news came in over the phone
that you did not have cancer, as they first thought,

I was in the kitchen trying to follow a recipe,
glancing from cookbook to stove,
shifting my glasses from my nose to my forehead and back,

a recipe, as it turned out, for ratatouille,
a complicated vegetable dish
which you or any other dog would turn up your nose at.

If you had been here, I imagine
you would have been curled up by the door
sleeping with your head resting on your tail.

And after I learned that you were not sick,
everything took on a different look
and appeared to be better than it usually is.

For example (and that's the first and last time
I will ever use those words in a poem),
I decided I should grate some cheese,

not even knowing if it was right for ratatouille,
and the sight of the cheese grater
with its red handle lying in the drawer

with all the other utensils made me marvel
at how this thing was so perfectly able and ready
to grate cheese just as you with your long smile

and your brown and white coat
are perfectly designed to be the dog you perfectly are.

Genesis

It was late, of course,
just the two of us still at the table
working on a second bottle of wine

when you speculated that maybe Eve came first
and Adam began as a rib
that leaped out of her side one paradisal afternoon.

Maybe, I remember saying,
because much was possible back then,
and I mentioned the talking snake
and the giraffes sticking their necks out of the ark,
their noses up in the pouring Old Testament rain.

I like a man with a flexible mind, you said then,
lifting your candlelit glass to me
and I raised mine to you and began to wonder

what life would be like as one of your ribs—
to be with you all the time,
riding under your blouse and skin,
caged under the soft weight of your breasts,

your favorite rib, I am assuming,
if you ever bothered to stop and count them

which is just what I did later that night
after you had fallen asleep
and we were fitted tightly back to front,
your long legs against the length of mine,
my fingers doing the crazy numbering that comes of love.

TWO

Horoscopes for the Dead

Every morning since you disappeared for good,
I read about you in the daily paper
along with the box scores, the weather, and all the bad news.

Some days I am reminded that today
will not be a wildly romantic time for you,
nor will you be challenged by educational goals,
nor will you need to be circumspect at the workplace.

Another day, I learn that you should not miss
an opportunity to travel and make new friends
though you never cared much about either.

I can't imagine you ever facing a new problem
with a positive attitude, but you will definitely not
be doing that, or anything like that, on this weekday in March.
And the same goes for the fun
you might have gotten from group activities,
a likelihood attributed to everyone under your sign.

A dramatic rise in income may be a reason
to treat yourself, but that would apply
more to all the Pisces who are still alive,
still swimming up and down the stream of life
or suspended in a pool in the shade of an overhanging tree.

But you will be relieved to learn
that you no longer need to reflect carefully before acting,
nor do you have to think more of others,
and never again will creative work take a back seat
to the business responsibilities that you never really had.

And don't worry today or any day
about problems caused by your unwillingness
to interact rationally with your many associates.
No more goals for you, no more romance,
no more money or children, jobs or important tasks,
but then again, you were never thus encumbered.

So leave it up to me now
to plan carefully for success and the wealth it may bring,
to value the dear ones close to my heart,
and to welcome any intellectual stimulation that comes my way
though that sounds like a lot to get done on a Tuesday.

I am better off closing the newspaper,
putting on the clothes I wore yesterday
(when I read that your financial prospects were looking up)
then pushing off on my copper-colored bicycle
and pedaling along the shore road by the bay.

And you stay just as you are,
lying there in your beautiful blue suit,
your hands crossed on your chest
like the wings of a bird who has flown
in its strange migration not north or south
but straight up from earth
and pierced the enormous circle of the zodiac.

Hell

I have a feeling that it is much worse
than shopping for a mattress at a mall,

of greater duration without question,
and there is no random pitchforking here,
no licking flames to fear,
only this cavernous store with its maze of bedding.

Yet wandering past the jovial kings,
the more sensible queens,
and the cheerless singles
no scarlet sheet will ever cover,

I am thinking of a passage from the *Inferno*,
which I could fully bring to mind
and recite in English or even Italian

if the salesman who has been following us—
a crumpled pack of Newports

visible in the pocket of his short sleeve shirt—
would stop insisting for a moment
that we test this one, then this softer one,

which we do by lying down side by side,
arms rigid, figures on a tomb,
powerless to imagine what it would be like

to sleep or love this way
under the punishing rows of fluorescent lights,
which Dante might have included
had he been able to lie on his back between us here today.

Simple Arithmetic

I spend a little time nearly every day
on a gray wooden dock
on the edge of a wide lake, thinly curtained by reeds.

And if there is nothing on my mind
but the motion of the wavelets
and the high shape-shifting of clouds,

I look out at the whole picture
and divide the scene into what was here
five hundred years ago and what was not.

Then I subtract all that was not here
and multiply everything that was by ten,
so when my calculations are complete,

all that remains is water and sky,
the dry sound of wind in the reeds,
and the sight of an unflappable heron on the shore.

All the houses are gone, and the boats
as well as the hedges and the walls,
the curving brick paths, and the distant siren.

The plane crossing the sky is no more
and the same goes for the swimming pools,
the furniture and the pastel umbrellas on the decks,

And the binoculars around my neck are also gone,
and so is the little painted dock itself—
according to my figuring—

and gone are my notebook and my pencil
and there I go, too,
erased by my own eraser and blown like shavings off the page.

Her

There is no noisier place than the suburbs,
someone once said to me
as we were walking along a fairway,
and every day is pleased to offer fresh evidence:

the chainsaw, the leaf-blower blowing
one leaf around an enormous house with columns,
on Mondays and Thursdays the garbage truck
equipped with air brakes, reverse beeper, and merciless grinder.

There's dogs, hammers, backhoes,
or serious earthmovers if today is not your day.
How can the birds get a peep
or a chirp in edgewise, I would like to know?

But this morning is different,
only a soft clicking sound
and the low talk of two workmen working
on the house next door, laying tile I am guessing.

Otherwise, all quiet for a change,
just the clicking of tiles being handled
and their talking back and forth in Spanish,
then one of them asking in English

"What was her name?" and the silence of the other.

Florida

This yellow rubber ducky
afloat in the middle of a blue-green pool
with its red beak and its tail up
is one of those duckies with sunglasses on,

a cool ducky, nonchalant
little dude on permanent vacation.
But this morning he looks different,
his shades more like the dark glasses of the blind

and him a poor sightless creature swiveling
on the surface of the ruffled water,
lost at a busy intersection of winds,
unable to see the cobalt-blue sky,

the fans of palmettos, or the bright pink hibiscus,
all much ablaze now in my unshielded, lucky eyes.

A Question About Birds

I am going to sit on a rock near some water
or on a slope of grass
under a high ceiling of white clouds,

and I am going to stop talking
so I can wander around in that spot
the way John James Audubon might have wandered

through a forest of speckled sunlight,
stopping now and then to lean
against an elm, mop his brow,

and listen to the songs of birds.
Did he wonder, as I often do,
how they regard the songs of other species?

Would it be like listening to the Chinese
merchants at an outdoor market?
Or do all the birds perfectly understand one another?

Or is that nervous chittering
I often hear from the upper branches
the sound of some tireless little translator?

The New Globe

It was a birthday gift,
the kind that comes on a stand
and glows from within at night.

It's the size of a basketball
but much more interesting
with all its multicolored countries

and its blue pelagic expanses.
No matter how closely you look,
you will not see a seabird or a fellow sitting on a wall,

yet place a hand on its curvature
and you will feel the raised mountain ranges,
the bumpy Himalayas under your palm.

It shows little desire to join the solar system,
content to remain in this room
showing one side of itself at a time.

And it is a small thrill to gaze upon it
as if gazing through space
from another planet or a balcony of clouds.

You can spin it on its famous axis
and stop it with a thumb
to see where you might belong in the world.

Or you can pretend, as I did,
that your index finger
would go down as the first index finger

in history to circumnavigate the earth.
Just don't get lost like me,
lost as a baby dropped in an ocean.

Oh it's a good thing I was alone,
nobody there to hear me shouting
The Cape of Good Hope must be somewhere, but where?

Girl

Only a few weeks ago,
the drawings you would bring in
were drawings of a tower with a fairy princess

leaning out from a high turret,
a swirl of stars in the background,
and bright moons, distant planets with rings.

Then yesterday you brought in
a drawing of a scallion,
a single scallion on a sheet of white paper—

another crucial step
along the path of human development,
I thought to myself

as I admired the slender green stalk,
the white bulb, and the little beard
of roots that you had penciled in so carefully.

Watercoloring

The sky began to tilt,
a shift of light toward the higher clouds,
so I seized my brush
and dipped my little cup in the stream,

but once I streaked the paper gray
with a hint of green,
water began to slide down the page,
rivulets looking for a river.

And again, I was too late—
then the sky made another turn,
this time as if to face a mirror
held in the outstretched arm of a god.

At the Home of the Baroness of Pembrokeshire

The bedroom that was mine for the night
was as delicate
as a room on a page in Flaubert.

The bedclothes were pulled so taut
I slept outside the covers
trying not to dream, trying to be invisible.

When I smoked a cigarette in the dark,
I flicked the ashes out the top
of a lowered bathroom window.

Whenever I crossed the room,
I feared the furniture
would shatter in the wake of my passing.

If one of the roses in the Chinese vase
is now less aromatic than the others,
blame it on the furtive sniff I took.

Tiptoeing down for breakfast,
I regretted only the pigeons I had let in
after all their bobbing and moaning on the sill.

Poem on the Three Hundredth
Anniversary of the Trinity School

When a man asked me to look back three hundred years
Over the hilly landscape of America,
I must have picked up the wrong pen,
The one that had no poem lurking in its vein of ink.

So I walked in circles for days like a blind horse
Harnessed to an oaken pole that turns a millstone,
A sight we might have seen so many years ago—
Barley being ground near a swift and silent millrace—

Which led to other sights of smoky battlefields,
The frames of houses, then a tall steeple by a thoroughfare,
Which I climbed and then could see even more,
A nation being built of logs and words, ideas, and wooden nails.

The greatest of my grandfathers was not visible,
And the house I live in was not a pasture yet,

Only a wooded hillside strewn with glacial rock,
Yet I could see Dutch men and women on an island without
    bridges.

And I saw winding through the scene a line of people,
Students it would seem from their satchels and jackets,
Three hundred of them, one for every school year
Walking single-file over the decades into the present.

I thought of the pages they had filled
With letters and numbers, the lifted bits of chalk,
The changing flag limp in the corner, the hand raised,
The learning eye brightening to a spark in the iris.

And then I heard their singing, all those voices
Joined in a fluid chorus, and all those years
Synchronized by the harmony of their anthem,
History now a single chord, and time its key and measure.

THREE

The Chairs That No One Sits In

You see them on porches and on lawns
down by the lakeside,
usually arranged in pairs implying a couple

who might sit there and look out
at the water or the big shade trees.
The trouble is you never see anyone

sitting in these forlorn chairs
though at one time it must have seemed
a good place to stop and do nothing for a while.

Sometimes there is a little table
between the chairs where no one
is resting a glass or placing a book facedown.

It may not be any of my business,
but let us suppose one day
that everyone who placed those vacant chairs

on a veranda or a dock sat down in them
if only for the sake of remembering
what it was they thought deserved

to be viewed from two chairs,
side by side with a table in between.
The clouds are high and massive on that day.

The woman looks up from her book.
The man takes a sip of his drink.
Then there is only the sound of their looking,

the lapping of lake water, and a call of one bird
then another, cries of joy or warning—
it passes the time to wonder which.

Memorizing "The Sun Rising" by John Donne

Every reader loves the way he tells off
the sun, shouting busy old fool
into the English skies even though they
were likely cloudy on that seventeenth-century morning.

And it's a pleasure to spend this sunny day
pacing the carpet and repeating the words,
feeling the syllables lock into rows
until I can stand and declare,
the book held closed by my side,
that hours, days, and months are but the rags of time.

But after a few steps into stanza number two,
wherein the sun is blinded by his mistress's eyes,
I can feel the first one begin to fade
like sky-written letters on a windy day.

And by the time I have taken in the third,
the second is likewise gone, a blown-out candle now,
a wavering line of acrid smoke.

So it's not until I leave the house
and walk three times around this hidden lake
that the poem begins to show
any interest in walking by my side.

Then, after my circling,
better than the courteous dominion
of her being all states and him all princes,

better than love's power to shrink
the wide world to the size of a bedchamber,

and better even than the compression
of all that into the rooms of these three stanzas

is how, after hours stepping up and down the poem,
testing the plank of every line,
it goes with me now, contracted into a little spot within.

Two Creatures

The last time I looked, the dog was lying
on the freshly cut grass
but now she has moved under the picnic table.

I wonder what causes her to shift
from one place to another,
to get up for no apparent reason from her spot

by the stove, scratch one ear,
then relocate, slumping down
on the other side of the room by the big window,

or I will see her hop onto the couch to nap
then later find her down
on the Turkish carpet, her nose in the fringe.

The moon rolls across the night sky
and stops to peer down at the earth,
and the dog rolls through these rooms

and onto the lawn, pausing here and there
to sleep or to stare up at me, head in her paws,
to consider the scentless pen in my hand

or the open book on my lap.
And because her eyes always follow me,
she must wonder, too, why

I shift from place to place,
from the couch to the sink
or the pencil sharpener on the wall—

two creatures bound by wonderment
though unlike her, I have never once worried
after letting her out the back door

that she would take off in the car
and leave me to die
behind the solid locked doors of this house.

Vocation

As I watched the night sky
from the wooden dock
I had painted gray earlier that day

I saw an airplane fly,
its red port-light blinking all the while,
right through the Big Dipper

nearly clipping one of the stars
of that constellation,
which was tilted upside-down at the time

and seemed to be pouring whatever it held
into space one big dipperful at a time.

And that was when I discovered
poised right above me
a hitherto unknown constellation

composed of six stars,
two for the snout and the four behind
for the pig's trotters

though it would have taken some time
to make anyone see that.

But since there was no one there
lying next to me,
my constellation of the Pig
remained a secret

and a bright reminder,
after many jumbled days and nights,
of my true vocation—

keeping an eye on things
whether they existed or not,
recumbent under the random stars.

My Unborn Children

... of all your children, only those who were born.
—Wisława Szymborska

I have so many of them I sometimes lose track,
several hundred last time I counted
but that was years ago.

I remember one was made of marble
and another looked like a penguin
some days and on other days a white flower.

Many of them appeared only in dreams
or while I was writing a poem
with freezing fingers in the house of a miser.

Others were more like me
looking out the window in a worn shirt
then later staring into the dark.

None of them ever made the lacrosse team,
but they all made me as proud
as I was on the day they failed to be born.

There is no telling—
maybe tonight or later in the week
another one of my children will not be born.

I see this next one as a baby
lying naked below a ceiling pasted with stars
but only for a little while,

then I see him as a monk in a gray robe
walking back and forth
in the gravel yard of an imaginary monastery,

his head bowed, wondering where I am.

Hangover

If I were crowned emperor this morning,
every child who is playing Marco Polo
in the swimming pool of this motel,
shouting the name Marco Polo back and forth

Marco   Polo   Marco   Polo

would be required to read a biography
of Marco Polo—a long one with fine print—
as well as a history of China and of Venice,
the birthplace of the venerated explorer

Marco   Polo   Marco   Polo

after which each child would be quizzed
by me then executed by drowning
regardless how much they managed
to retain about the glorious life and times of

Marco   Polo   Marco   Polo

Table Talk

Not long after we had sat down to dinner
at a long table in a restaurant in Chicago
and were deeply engrossed in the heavy menus,
one of us—a bearded man with a colorful tie—
asked if anyone had ever considered
applying the paradoxes of Zeno to the martyrdom
    of St. Sebastian.

The differences between these two figures
were much more striking than the differences
between the Cornish hen and the trout amandine
I was wavering between, so I looked up and closed my menu.

If, the man with the tie continued,
an object moving through space
will never reach its destination because it is always
limited to cutting the distance to its goal in half,

then it turns out that St. Sebastian did not die

from the wounds inflicted by the arrows:

the cause of death was fright at the spectacle of their approach.

Saint Sebastian, according to Zeno, would have died

    of a heart attack.

I think I'll have the trout, I told the waiter,

for it was now my turn to order,

but all through the elegant dinner

I kept thinking of the arrows forever nearing

the pale, quivering flesh of St. Sebastian,

a fleet of them forever halving the tiny distances

to his body, tied to a post with rope,

even after the archers had packed it in and gone home.

And I thought of the bullet never reaching

the wife of William Burroughs, an apple trembling on her head,

the tossed acid never getting to the face of that girl,

and the Oldsmobile never knocking my dog into a ditch.

The theories of Zeno floated above the table

like thought balloons from the 5th century before Christ,

yet my fork continued to arrive at my mouth

delivering morsels of asparagus and crusted fish,

and after we ate and lifted our glasses,
we left the restaurant and said goodbye on the street
then walked our separate ways in the world where things
    do arrive,

where people usually get where they are going—
where trains pull into the station in a cloud of vapor,
where geese land with a splash on the surface of a pond,
and the one you love crosses the room and arrives in your
    arms—

and, yes, where sharp arrows can pierce a torso,
splattering blood on the groin and the feet of the saint,

that popular subject of European religious painting.
One hagiographer compared him to a hedgehog bristling
    with quills.

Delivery

Moon in the upper window,
shadow of my crooked pen on the page,
and I find myself wishing that the news of my death

might be delivered not by a dark truck
but by a child's attempt to draw that truck—
the long rectangular box of the trailer,

some lettering on the side,
then the protruding cab, the ovoid wheels,
maybe the inscrutable profile of a driver,

and puffs of white smoke
issuing from the tailpipe, drawn like flowers
and similar in their expression to the clouds in the sky,
    only smaller.

The Symbol

Once upon a time there were two oval mirrors
hanging face to face
on the walls of a local barbershop

in the capital city of a country
running the length of a valley
lined with the stubborn molars of mountains.

It's hard to say how the mirrors felt
about all the faces peering into them—
the unshorn, the clean-cut, and the bald—

their only job being to double
whatever stands in front of them
including the cologned heads of customers.

And when business was slow
the mirrors would see the barbers themselves
glancing in to run a comb quickly through their hair.

Every day except Sunday the mirrors
received the rounded heads
and gave back the news, good or bad.

And the reward for their patience
arrived at night in the empty shop
when they could look down the long

corridors of each other—
one looking at the dead mirrors of the past,
the other looking into the unborn mirrors of the future,

which means that the barbershop
must symbolize the present, in case anyone wants to know—
the present with its razors, towels, and chairs,

its green awning withdrawn,
its big window and motionless pole,
and the two mirrors who lived repetitively ever after.

Winter in Utah

The road across a wide snowy valley
could not have been straighter
if someone had drawn it with a ruler

which someone probably did on a table
in a surveyor's office a century ago
with a few other men looking over his shoulder.

We're out in the middle of nowhere, you said,
as we bisected the whitened fields—
a few dark bison here and there

and I remember two horses snorting by a shed—
or maybe a little southwest of nowhere,
you added, after you unfolded a map of the state.

But that night, after speeding on sleds
down a road of ice, the sky packed with stars,
and the headlights of our host's truck blazing behind,

it seemed we had come a little closer to somewhere.
And in the morning with the snow sparkling
and the rough white mountains looming,

a magpie flashed up from a fence post,
all black and white in its airy exertions,
and I said good morning to him

on this first day of the new decade
all of which left me to wonder
if we had not arrived at the middle of exactly where we were.

What She Said

When he told me he expected me to pay for dinner,
I was like give me a break.

I was not the exact equivalent of give me a break.
I was just similar to give me a break.

As I said, I was like give me a break.

I would love to tell you
how I was able to resemble give me a break
without actually being identical to give me a break,

but all I can say is that I sensed
a similarity between me and give me a break.

And that was close enough
at that point in the evening

even if it meant I would fall short
of standing up from the table and screaming
give me a break,

for God's sake will you please give me a break?!

No, for that moment
with the rain streaking the restaurant windows
and the waiter approaching,

I felt the most I could be was like

to a certain degree

give me a break.

Feedback

The woman who wrote from Phoenix
after my reading there

to tell me they were all still talking about it

just wrote again
to tell me that they had stopped.

Drawing You from Memory

I seem to have forgotten several features
crucial to the doing of this,
for instance, how your lower lip
meets your upper lip besides just being below it,
and what happens at the end of the nose,
how much does it shade the plane of your cheek,
and would even a bit of nostril be visible from this angle?
Chinese eyes, you call them
which could be the difficulty I have
in showing the flash of light in your iris,
and being so far away from you for so long,
I cannot remember what direction
it flows, the deep river of your hair.

But all of this will come together
the minute I see you again at the station,
my notebook and pens packed away,
your face smiling as I cup it in my hands,

or frowning later when we are home
and you are berating me in the kitchen
waving the pages in my face
demanding to know the name of this latest little whore.

Riverside, California

I would have to say that the crown
resting on the head of my first acid trip
was the moment I went down on one knee
backstage at the Top Hat Lounge
and proposed marriage to all three of the Ikettes.

We had no idea, Tom and I,
that the Ike and Tina Turner Revue would be playing there
when we stepped out for some lights and drinks,
but sometimes the tortoise gets lucky, they say,
and comes across an opening in the chain-link fence.

With many people sending many drinks
to our maniacally happy table,
how could I not feel that I had slipped
out of the enclosure of the past
where I used to inch in circles through the grass
when I wasn't sunning myself on a favorite rock?

So the night flew on with its mighty colors
until there emerged a posture
of valor and chivalric intensity
as the music, especially "Nutbush City Limits,"
became more beautiful and fair, like a bower in a poem.

And even better was the sound
I heard when it became clear to those girls
why I had appeared backstage during a break.

Yes, the best was the laughter
of those three backup singers
in their shiny wigs and short red sequin dresses—

their sweet mocking laughter
at my courteous sincerity, my ardor,
after I had breached their dressing room
and descended to one knee before them all.

FOUR

Cemetery Ride

My new copper-colored bicycle
is looking pretty fine under a blue sky
as I pedal along one of the sandy paths
in the Palm Cemetery here in Florida,

wheeling past the headstones of the Lyons,
the Campbells, the Dunlaps, and the Davenports,
Arthur and Ethel who outlived him by 11 years
I slow down even more to notice,

but not so much as to fall sideways on the ground.
And here's a guy named Happy Grant
next to his wife Jean in their endless bed.
Annie Sue Simms is right there and sounds

a lot more fun than Theodosia S. Hawley.
And good afternoon, Emily Polasek
and to you too, George and Jane Cooper,
facing each other in profile, two sides of a coin.

I wish I could take you all for a ride
in my wire basket on this glorious April day,
not a thing as simple as your name, Bill Smith,
even trickier than Clarence Augustus Coddington.

Then how about just you, Enid Parker?
Would you like to gather up your voluminous skirts
and ride sidesaddle on the crossbar
and tell me what happened between 1863 and 1931?

I'll even let you ring the silver bell.
But if you're not ready, I can always ask
Mary Brennan to rise from her long sleep
beneath the swaying gray beards of Spanish moss

and ride with me along these halls of the dead
so I can listen to her strange laughter
as some crows flap in the blue overhead
and the spokes of my wheels catch the dazzling sun.

Thank-You Notes

Under the vigilant eye of my mother
I had to demonstrate my best penmanship
by thanking Uncle Gerry for the toy soldiers—

little red members of the Coldstream Guards—
and thanking Aunt Helen for the pistol and holster,

but now I am writing other notes
alone at a small cherry desk
with a breeze coming in an open window,

thanking everyone I happened to see
on my long walk to the post office today

and anyone who ever gave me directions
or placed a hand on my shoulder,
or cut my hair or fixed my car.

And while I am at it,
thanks to everyone who happened to die
on the same day that I was born.

Thank you for stepping aside to make room for me,
for giving up your seat,
getting out of the way, to be blunt.

I waited until almost midnight
on that day in March before I appeared,
all slimy and squinting, in order to leave time

for enough of the living
to drive off a bridge or collapse in a hallway
so that I could enter without causing a stir.

So I am writing now to thank everyone
who drifted off that day
like smoke from a row of blown-out candles—
for giving up your only flame.

One day, I will follow your example
and step politely out of the path
of an oncoming infant, but not right now

with the subtropical sun warming this page
and the wind stirring the fronds of the palmettos,

and me about to begin another note
on my very best stationery
to the ones who are making room today

for the daily host of babies,
descending like bees with their wings and stingers,
ready to get busy with all their earthly joys and tasks.

Lakeside

As optical illusions go
it was one of the more spectacular,
a cluster of bright stars
appearing to move along the night sky
as if on a secret mission

while, of course, it was the low clouds
that were doing the moving,
scattered over my head by a wind from the east.
And as hard as I looked
I could not get the stars to budge again.

It was like the curious figure
of the duck/rabbit—
why, even paradoxical Wittgenstein
could not find his way back to the rabbit
once he had beheld the bill of the duck.

But which was which?
Were the stars the rabbit
and the blown clouds the duck?
or the other way around?
You're being ridiculous,

I said to myself,
on the walk back to the house,
but then the correct answer struck me
not like a bolt of lightning,
but more like a heavy bolt of cloth.

Revision

When I finally pulled onto the shoulder
of a long country road

after driving a few hundred miles
without stopping or even blinking,

I sat there long enough to count
twenty-four cows in a wide, sloping pasture.

Nothing about the scene asked to be changed,
things being just what they were,

and there was even a green hill
looming solidly in the background.

Still, I felt the urge
to find a pencil and edit one of them out,

that swaybacked one standing
in the shade in a far corner of the field.

I was too young then to see
that she was staring into the great mystery

just as intently as her sisters,
her gorgeous, brown and white, philosophic sisters.

Night and Day

Funny how that works,
the breathing all day then it continuing
into the night
when I am absent from the company of the wakeful
oblivious even to the bedroom windows
and the ghost dance of the curtains
but still breathing
and turning in bed
pulling the covers tight around me
maybe caught in the irons of a dream,
like that one about the birds, but
more like an evil society of birds
a kind of neighborhood watch group
throwing a block party
with the usual balloons and folding chairs
and tables covered with covered dishes
and many children running
in circles or jagged lines
only everyone with bird heads, bigger than life,

even the children with bird heads
and yes, you guessed it
the birds up in the trees
have little human faces
and they are all talking amongst themselves
about the cloudy weather
and the bushes laden with berries
as if none of it were the least bit funny.

My Hero

Just as the hare is zipping across the finish line,
the tortoise has stopped once again
by the roadside,
this time to stick out his neck
and nibble a bit of sweet grass,
unlike the previous time
when he was distracted
by a bee humming in the heart of a wildflower.

The Meatball Department

There is no such thing as a meatball department
as far as anyone knows.
No helpful clerk has ever answered the question
where do you keep your meatballs?
by pointing to the back of the store
and saying you'll find them over there in the meatball
    department.

We don't have to narrow it down
to Swedish and Italian meatballs to know
that meatballs are already too specific
to have an entire department named after them
unlike Produce, Appliances, or Ladies' Shoes.

It's like when you get angry at me
for reading in bed with the light on
when you are trying to fall asleep,
I cannot find a department for that.

Like meatballs, it's too small a thing to have its own
    department
unlike Rudeness and Selfishness which are located
down various aisles of the store known as Marriage.

I should just turn off the light
but instead I have stopped in that vast store
and I will now climb into my cart,
clasp my knees against my chest and wait
for the manager or some other person of authority

to push me down to the police station
or just out to the parking lot,
otherwise known as the department of lost husbands,
or sometimes, as now, the department of dark and pouring rain.

Silhouette

There is a kind of sweet pointlessness
that can visit at any time,
say this afternoon when I find myself
rustling around in the woods behind the house

and making with my right hand
the head of a duck,
the kind that would cast a silhouetted
profile on a white screen
in a darkened room with a single source of light
if one were in the mood to entertain.

But I am outdoors today and this duck
has a wrist for a neck
and fingers for a beak that never stops flapping,
jabbering about some duck topic,
unless I rotate my arm and let him face me.

Then he stops his quacking
and listens to what I have to say,
even cocking his head like a dog
that listens all day to his master speaking
in English or Turkish or Albanian.

There was talk of war this morning
on the radio, and I imagined the treads of tanks
churning over the young trees again
and planes hacking the air to pieces,
but there is nothing I can do about that
except to continue my walk in the woods
conversing with my hand—

so benign an activity that if everyone
did this perhaps there would *be* no wars,
I might say in a speech
to the ladies' auxiliary of the Future Farmers
    of America.

And now it is getting to be evening,
a shift from blue to violet
behind the bare staves of trees.
It is also my birthday,
but there is nothing I can do about that either—

cannot control the hands of time
like this hand in the shape of this duck
who peers out of my sleeve
with its beak of fingers, its eye of air.

No—I am doing no harm,
nor am I doing much good.

Would any bridge span a river?
would a college of nurses have ever been founded?
would one stone ever be placed on top of another
if people were concerned with nothing
but the shadows cast by nonexistent ducks?

So the sky darkens as always,
and now I am tripping over the fallen branches
as I head back downhill
toward the one burning light in the house
while the duck continues its agitated talk,
in my pocket now,
excited about his fugitive existence,
awed by his sudden and strange life
as each of us should be, one and all.

But never mind that, I think,
as I grab the young trees with my other hand,
braking my way down,
one boot in front of the other,
ready for my birthday dinner,
my birthday sleep, and my crazy birthday dreams.

Bread and Butter

You could hear the ocean from my room
in the guesthouse where I often stayed,
that constant, distant, washy rumbling under the world.

I would sometimes slide back the glass door
and stand on the deck in a thin robe
just to be under the stars again or under the clouds

and to hear more clearly the dogs
on the property barking—the brave mother and her pups,
all white, bearded, and low to the ground.

And now something tells me I should make
more out of all that, moving down
and inward where a poem is meant to go.

But this time I want to leave it be,
the sea, the stars, the dogs, and the clouds—
just written down, folded in fours, and handed to my host.

Roses

In those weeks of midsummer
when the roses in gardens begin to give up,
the big red, white, and pink ones—
the inner, enfolded petals growing cankerous,
the ones at the edges turning brown
or fallen already, down on their girlish backs
in the rough beds of turned-over soil,

then how terrible the expressions on their faces,
a kind of *was it all really worth it?* look,
to die here slowly in front of everyone
in the garden of a bed-and-breakfast
in a provincial English market town,
to expire by degrees of corruption
in plain sight of all the neighbors passing by,

the thin mail carrier, the stocky butcher
(thank God the children pay no attention),
the swiveling faces in the windows of the buses,

and now this stranger staring over the wall,
his hair disheveled, a scarf loose around his neck,
writing in a notebook, writing about us no doubt,
about how terrible we look under the punishing sun.

After I Heard You Were Gone

I sat for a while on a bench in the park.
It was raining lightly but this was not a movie
even though a couple hurried by,
the girl holding his jacket over her head,
and the chess players were gathering up their pieces
and fanning out into the streets.

No, this was something different.
I could have sworn the large oak trees
had just appeared there overnight.
And that pigeon looked as if
it had once been a playing card
that a magician had transformed with the flick of a scarf.

On Reading a Program Note
on Aaron Copland

How admirable, yet futile,

to be born in Brooklyn in 1900
and to die in North Tarrytown in 1990

to spend all those years inching northward
over the rough pavements of the city

then into the open fields
and through dark woods, cold streams.

So many steadfast hours,
inside his pale, brittle shell—

nine decades
of snail-like perseverance!

Poetry Workshop Held in a
Former Cigar Factory in Key West

After our final class, when we disbanded
as the cigar rollers here had disbanded decades ago,
getting up from their benches for the last time
as the man who read to them during their shift
closed his book without marking the page where he left off,
I complimented myself on my restraint.

For never in that sunny white building
did I draw an analogy between cigar-making and poetry.
Not even after I had studied the display case
containing the bladed *chaveta*, the ring gauge,
and the hand guillotine with its measuring rule
did I suggest that the cigar might be a model for the poem.

Nor did I ever cite the exemplary industry
of those anonymous rollers and cutters—
the best producing 300 cigars in a day
compared to 3 flawless poems in a lifetime if you're lucky—

who worked the broad leaves of tobacco
into cylinders ready to be held lightly in the hand.

Not once did I imply that tightly rolling an intuition
into a perfectly shaped, handmade thing
might encourage a reader to remove the brightly colored
encircling band and slip it over her finger
and take the poet as her spouse in a sudden puff of smoke.
No, I kept all of that to myself, until now.

Returning the Pencil to Its Tray

Everything is fine—
the first bits of sun are on
the yellow flowers behind the low wall,

people in cars are on their way to work,
and I will never have to write again.

Just looking around
will suffice from here on in.

Who said I had to always play
the secretary of the interior?

And I am getting good at being blank,
staring at all the zeroes in the air.

It must have been all the time spent
in the kayak this summer
that brought this out,

the yellow one which went
nicely with the pale blue life jacket—

the sudden, tippy
buoyancy of the launch,
then the exertion, striking
into the wind against the short waves,

but the best was drifting back,
the paddle resting athwart the craft,
and me mindless in the middle of time.

Not even that dark cormorant
perched on the *No Wake* sign,
his narrow head raised
as if he were looking over something,

not even that inquisitive little fellow
could bring me to write another word.

Acknowledgments

The author is grateful to the editors of the following journals, where some of these poems first appeared:

The Atlantic: "Cemetery Ride," "Grave"

Boulevard: "After I Heard You Were Gone," "Florida"

Cimarron Review: "Two Creatures"

Crazyhorse: "Drawing You from Memory," "Thieves"

Five Points: "Genesis," "Riverside, California," "The Meatball Department"

The Gettysburg Review: "Gold"

Gulf Coast: "Bread and Butter"

Knockout: "Night and Day"

London Review of Books: "The Guest," "Lakeside"

The New Yorker: "Table Talk"

Oxford American: "The Flâneur"

The Paris Review: "Returning the Pencil to Its Tray"

PEN America 12: Correspondences: "Horoscopes for the Dead"

Poetry: "The Chairs That No One Sits In," "Her," "Memorizing 'The Sun Rising' by John Donne"

Poetry East: "Palermo"

Poetry Review (U.K.): "Silhouette"

Open City: "What She Said," "Thank-You Notes"

Oranges & Sardines: "Revision"

Real Simple: "The Straightener"

Slate: "The Symbol"

The Southampton Review: "Hangover," "My Unborn Children," "Girl," "Poetry Workshop Held in a Former Cigar Factory in Key West"

The Southern Review: "A Question About Birds"

Subtropics: "As Usual," "Delivery"

Superstition Review: "My Hero"

Tundra: "Hell"

"Grave" was selected by Amy Gerstler to appear in *Best American Poetry 2010* (Scribner) and was also included in *Best Spiritual Writing 2011*, edited by Philip Zaleski (Penguin).

I am grateful to many people at Random House, especially David Ebershoff, whose steady editorial hand and abiding enthusiasm made this book a reality. Thanks also to Chris Calhoun for his support and our uplifting friendship, and to George Green, who assigned most of these poems a passing grade.

PHOTO: © STEVEN KOVICH

Billy Collins is the author of a number of poetry collections, including *Ballistics, The Trouble with Poetry and Other Poems, Nine Horses, Sailing Alone Around the Room, Questions About Angels, The Apple That Astonished Paris, The Art of Drowning, Picnic, Lightning,* and *Aimless Love.* He is also the editor of *Poetry 180: A Turning Back to Poetry; 180 More: Extraordinary Poems for Every Day;* and *Bright Wings: An Illustrated Anthology of Poems About Birds.* A distinguished professor of English at Lehman College of the City University of New York, he served as Poet Laureate of the United States from 2001 to 2003 and Poet Laureate of New York State from 2004 to 2006.

From bestselling author and former
United States Poet Laureate

BILLY COLLINS

"A poet of plenitude, irony, and Augustan grace."
—*The New Yorker*

SAILING ALONE AROUND THE ROOM

Billy Collins offers the lyric equivalent of an album of Greatest Hits in this landmark collection of poems, both new and selected from four earlier collections, which secured for him a national reputation.

NINE HORSES

These poems are quiet meditations grounded in everyday life that ascend effortlessly into eye-opening imaginative realms. Billy Collins continues his delicate negotiation between the clear and the mysterious in *Nine Horses*.

THE TROUBLE WITH POETRY

The Trouble with Poetry explores boyhood, jazz, love, the passage of time, and writing—themes familiar to Billy Collins's fans. Gorgeous, funny, and deeply empathetic, Collins's poetry is a window through which we see our lives.

BALLISTICS

In this moving and playful collection, Billy Collins touches on an array of subjects—love, death, solitude, youth, and aging—delving deeper than ever before into the intricate folds of life.

HOROSCOPES FOR THE DEAD

Billy Collins's verbal gifts are on full display in this smart, lyrical, and mischievous collection of poetry, which covers the everlasting themes of love and loss, youth and aging, and solitude and union.

POETRY 180

Inspired by Billy Collins's poem-a-day program with the Library of Congress, *Poetry 180* is the perfect anthology for readers and teachers who want to bring a new poem into their lives or classrooms every day.

180 MORE

In *180 More*, Billy Collins continues his mission of exposing readers of all ages to today's poetry. Here are another 180 hospitable, engaging, reader-friendly poems, offering surprise and delight in a wide range of literary voices.

Random House Trade Paperbacks and eBooks